NATIONAL GEOGRAPHIC

The Iroquois

People of the Northeast

A HISTORICAL LOOK AT NATIVE AMERICANS

Ruby Maile

Produced through the worldwide resources of the National Geographic Society, John M. Fahey, Jr., President and Chief Executive Officer; Gilbert M. Grosvenor, Chairman of the Board; Nina D. Hoffman, Executive Vice President and President, Books and Education Publishing Group.

PREPARED BY NATIONAL GEOGRAPHIC SCHOOL PUBLISHING
Ericka Markman, Senior Vice President and President, Children's Books and Education Publishing Group; Steve Mico, Vice President and Editorial Director; Marianne Hiland, Executive Editor; Richard Easby, Editorial Manager; Jim Hiscott, Design Manager; Kristin Hanneman, Illustrations Manager; Matt Wascavage, Manager of Publishing Services; Sean Philpotts, Production Manager.

EDITORIAL MANAGEMENT
Morrison BookWorks, LLC

PROGRAM CONSULTANTS
Dr. Shirley V. Dickson, Program Director, Literacy, Education Commission of the States; Margit E. McGuire, Ph.D., Professor of Teacher Education and Social Studies, Seattle University.

CONTENT REVIEWER
Michael Galban, member of the Washoe-N. Paiute Nation; Interpretative Programs, Ganandogan State Historic Site, New York.

National Geographic Theme Sets program developed by Macmillan Education Australia, Pty Limited.

Published by the National Geographic Society
1145 17th Street, N.W.
Washington, D.C. 20036-4688

ISBN: 0-7922-4728-0

Product 41968

Printed in Hong Kong.

2008 2007 2006 2005
2 3 4 5 6 7 8 9 10 11 12 13 14 15

Contents

A Historical Look at Native Americans

Native Americans have lived in the United States for thousands of years, long before other peoples made their homes here. There are many different Native American nations or peoples, each with their own language, traditions, and way of life. These peoples include the Nez Perce, the Pueblos, the Iroquois, and the Cheyenne.

Key Concepts ....

1. The homelands of native people have influenced their food, clothing, and shelter.

2. The stories and arts of native people were an expression of culture and a way of passing on values.

3. Early trade was a way of exchanging both goods and ideas.

Native American Homelands of Long Ago

The Nez Perce

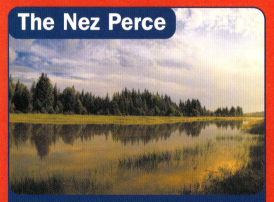

The Nez Perce lived along the rivers of the Northwest.

The Pueblos

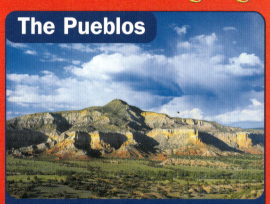

The Pueblos lived in the Southwest.

This Iroquois man is wearing ceremonial dress. In this book you will read about the history of the Iroquois people.

The Iroquois

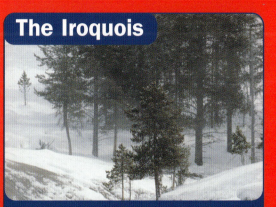

The Iroquois lived surrounded by the woods of the Northeast.

The Cheyenne

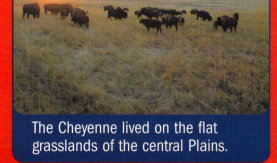

The Cheyenne lived on the flat grasslands of the central Plains.

The IROQUOIS:
People of the Northeast

The Iroquois are a group of Native American nations. The Iroquois lived south and east of Lake Ontario. This area is now upstate New York. French settlers named these people the Iroquois, but they prefer the name Haudenosaunee. The word means "people of the longhouse." The name comes from the houses the people lived in.

The Iroquois are a group of five nations, the Mohawk, Cayuga, Onondaga, Oneida, and Seneca. Once, these people were at war with each other. But they made peace and came together to form the Iroquois Confederacy, also called the **League** of Five Nations. The League was formed around 1570.

Although each nation had its own beliefs, all followed the laws of the League. The most important was the Great Law of Peace. It said that the Iroquois should not kill each other. In 1722, another nation called the Tuscarora joined the Iroquois Confederacy, making it the League of Six Nations.

The Homeland of the Iroquois

The original **homeland** of the Iroquois was the woodland of the Northeast. This land was covered with dense forests of pine, oak, maple, and ash. The Iroquois used the wood from the trees in many different ways. For example, they used it to make houses, canoes, and food containers such as bowls. The forests also had many rivers, lakes, and streams. They were surrounded by hills. The winters in the Iroquois homeland were severe, but the summers were warm.

Many Iroquois groups still live in the Northeast.

homeland
the place a people or nation chooses to make its home

Location of Iroquois Homeland

N
W E
S

Lake Ontario

NEW YORK

Key
Iroquois homeland

Food

The Iroquois got much of their food from the forests and rivers that surrounded them. The men went hunting and fishing. Both men and women gathered berries, fruits, and nuts.

Farming The Iroquois lived in an area where there was plenty of rainfall. This meant they were able to grow many crops.

Iroquois women looked after the fields. The women sowed the seeds and picked all the crops. They grew beans, corn, and squash. They called these crops "the three sisters." The three plants shared the land and grew well together. The Iroquois women planted the corn seeds first. When the corn started sprouting, the women sowed bean seeds. The bean plant is a climber, so it twined around the cornstalks as it grew. Next, the women planted squash around the bean plants. The squash plants spread across the ground and stopped weeds from growing.

These Iroquois women are sorting and grinding corn kernels.

Hunting and Fishing The main job of Iroquois men was to fish and hunt. They fished the many lakes and streams around where they lived. Often they planned fishing trips or **expeditions** to the Great Lakes. These expeditions could last up to one month. The fishing was best in the spring and the fall.

In the fall, the men left their villages to go hunting in the forest. They hunted game birds like the goose, the heron, and the turkey. They also hunted animals such as the bear and the beaver. However, their main goal was always to hunt deer. The deer was important because every part of it was used by the Iroquois.

The Iroquois used every part of the deer.

Iroquois Food Sources

Food Source	Work of Men	Work of Women
Fishing	✔	
Hunting	✔	
Farming		✔
Gathering	✔	✔

Clothing

The early Iroquois wore clothing to suit the seasons. In the Northeast, the summers are warm, but the winters are often very cold. The Iroquois used animal fur and hides from their hunting to make warm clothing. They also made clothing from plant **fibers**. Plants were also used to make dye to color the clothes.

Both the men and the women wore **moccasins** on their feet in winter. The moccasins were made of leather. People also wore fur-lined robes. They used porcupine quills to decorate their clothes and moccasins.

Men's Clothing Iroquois men wore deerskin skirts and leggings. In winter, they also wore deerskin shirts for warmth. In summer, they wore a **breechcloth** woven from plant fiber. All of these were decorated with porcupine quills, beads, and shells. The men also wore headgear decorated with beads, quills, shells, fur, and feathers.

This Iroquois man is wearing headgear decorated with feathers and fur.

Women's Clothing Iroquois women wore deerskin dresses. Sometimes they wore sashes around their waists. One type of dress was the overdress, a dress that can be worn over other clothes. The women wore deerskin skirts and leggings with the overdress. The skirts and leggings were decorated with beads and shells.

This Iroquois woman is wearing leggings, a skirt, and an overdress, all with traditional beading on them.

Shelter

The Iroquois lived in villages surrounded by fields. They stayed in one place because they were able to grow much of their food there. The nearby forests provided trees from which they built houses called **longhouses**.

Iroquois longhouses were long buildings. Some were more than 200 feet (57 meters) long. These houses were made to last a long time. They were made with wooden poles which were tied together and covered with sheets of bark. The bark covering kept out the wind and rain. Each longhouse also had holes in the roof to let smoke out and daylight in.

Longhouses had a long hallway with rooms on both sides. Many families shared a longhouse. Each family had its own space. Sleeping **platforms** and shelves lined the walls. The platforms had reed mats and deerskins on them to make them warm and comfortable. The shelves were higher up. They were used for storing baskets, pots, and the skins of animals.

Longhouses kept the Iroquois warm and dry during long, cold winters.

Key Concept 2 The stories and arts of native people were an expression of culture and a way of passing on values.

Language and Storytelling

Language helped bring the nations of the Iroquois League together. Even though the Iroquois nations spoke different languages, many people could speak all of the languages.

The Iroquois had no written language. Instead, they used speeches and storytelling to preserve the history and **culture** of the nations. Stories were passed down through generations.

> **culture**
> the traditions, language, dress, ceremonies, and other ways of life that a group of people share

The storytellers of some Iroquois nations would point to parts of a belt to tell a story. These belts had patterns made with shell beads called **wampum** beads. Each pattern meant something different. For example, a bundle of arrows was a sign of friendship. Snakes were a sign of darkness and danger.

Many wampum belts were like official records. No pledge or **treaty** was considered valid until wampum belts had been exchanged. The belts were exchanged at marriages and to seal political agreements.

The patterns on wampum belts were used to tell a story.

Arts and Crafts

Besides using wampum beads to make belts, the Iroquois also used them to decorate clothing. Shirts, breechcloths, leggings, robes, and moccasins were all decorated with beads.

Today, Iroquois people still make beaded items like this hat.

The Iroquois were also known for basket making, using wood from the black ash tree. After cutting down a tree, the Iroquois pounded the trunk with a mallet to get thin strips of wood called splints. As they pounded the tree trunks, the splints peeled off. The Iroquois twisted or wove these splints into the shape of a basket. Sometimes they used dyes to color the splints.

The Iroquois also created art from the husks, or outer covering, of corn. They coiled, braided, twined, and sewed the husks to make mats, masks, shoes, and baskets. They also used cornhusks to make both boy and girl dolls.

Dollmakers braided or twisted the husks to make the body, arms, and legs of a doll. They used corn-silk, the silky fibers that grow around corn, for hair. Sometimes they dressed the dolls in dyed husks or animal skin. They always left the doll's face blank, with no features such as eyes, nose, or mouth.

Key Concept 3 Early trade was a way of exchanging both goods and ideas.

Trade

Trade occurred frequently among the Iroquois nations and later with Europeans. The Iroquois traded **goods** and ideas with other Native Americans as well.

Trade between Native Americans Because the soil was **fertile** and they had plenty of water, the Iroquois could grow extra crops, such as corn, to trade. They traded with eastern peoples for wampum shells and with northern peoples for fur. Sometimes they traded by giving gifts to another group. The group would then give gifts in return.

trade
the buying, selling, or exchange of products

goods
Products that can be bought, sold, or exchanged

An Iroquois man holding a wampum belt

Trade with Europeans The Iroquois began trading with Europeans in the early sixteenth century. This contact changed Iroquois ideas about trade. Europeans wanted a lot of fur. At first, the Iroquois traded the fur of animals they caught. They traded it for goods such as guns, iron tools and pots, and glass beads. But soon they had killed off most of the fur-bearing animals on their land. Then they began to act as **middlemen**. A middleman is someone who buys goods from one person and sells them to another. The Iroquois traded their crops, such as corn, with other groups for beaver fur and then traded this fur with Europeans.

Later, the Iroquois began to look for more land where they could hunt for beavers. They began to drive other Native American people off this land. Over time, the Iroquois hunted so many beavers that beavers became very scarce in the new land. The fur trade eventually ended for the Iroquois.

A European felt hat made out of beaver fur

Think about what you read. Think about the pictures and charts. Use these to answer the questions. Share what you think with others.

1. How did the homeland of the Native Americans affect their life there?

2. Why was storytelling important?

3. What was special about the culture, or way of life, of this Native American group?

4. How did trade affect the Native American group discussed in this book?

Comparison Chart

A chart allows you to find specific facts quickly and easily.
You can learn new ideas without having to read many words.
Charts use words and a box-like layout to present ideas.

There are different kinds of charts.
This chart of Iroquois clothing is a comparison chart. It compares
different types of clothing and what they were made of.

How to Read a Comparison Chart

1. Read the title.

The title tells you the subject, or what the chart is about.

2. Read the column headings.

Columns go from top to bottom. The heading at the top of each
column tells you what kind of information is in the column.

3. Read the row headings.

Rows go from side to side. The headings in the left column name
items you will get information about as you read across each row.

4. Connect the information as you read.

Read across each row to find information about a subject. Read
down each column to compare information.

Iroquois Clothing

Type of Clothing	Deerskin	Fur	Plant Fiber	Porcupine Quills	Beads	Feathers	Shells
Shirts	✔	✔		✔	✔		✔
Dresses	✔		✔	✔	✔	✔	
Skirts	✔			✔	✔		✔
Breechcloths	✔		✔	✔	✔		✔
Leggings	✔			✔	✔		✔
Robes	✔	✔		✔	✔	✔	✔
Moccasins	✔	✔	✔	✔			✔
Headgear		✔		✔	✔	✔	✔

What's in the Chart?

Read the chart by following the steps on page 18. Write a few sentences about Iroquois clothing. Compare your sentences with what another student wrote.

Biographical Sources

The purpose of **biographical sources** is to give information about people's lives.

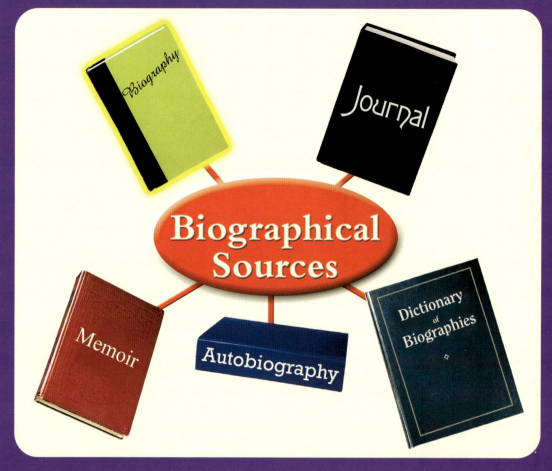

We read different biographical sources for different reasons. For example, if you want to read the story of someone's life, read a **biography**. But if you want to read one person's account of his or her own life, read that person's **autobiography**. Journals and memoirs are forms of autobiographies.

Iroquois Biographies

A biography tells the story of a person's life. The story is often told in the order in which things happened. This order is called chronological order. The following biographies are of Iroquois people.

Joseph Brant (1742–1807)

> **Name** of the person

> **Dates** tell of birth and death.

Joseph Brant

> Photographs and **illustrations** show the person at various times in his or her life.

Like many Native American leaders, Joseph Brant is well known for trying to save his people's land. He is also known for taking the side of the British in the American War of Independence. During his lifetime, this Mohawk chief took part in some well-known battles and traveled to England to meet British politicians. In the end, he helped his people keep some of their land.

Joseph Brant was born in 1742 on the banks of the Ohio River. His native name was Thayendanegea, which means "he places two bets."

> **Text** has details about the person's life.

Joseph Brant belonged to the Mohawk, one of the Iroquois nations. He lived at a time after Europeans had settled in North America.

When he was about 13, Brant was chosen by Sir William Johnson to attend a charity school for Native Americans. Sir William was an Englishman who was in charge of Indian affairs in the Northeast. While working with the Iroquois, Johnson became close to the Mohawk.

When fighting broke out between the British and the French over control of land in this part of North America, Brant went into battle. This war is called the French and Indian War. Some Native American groups fought on the side of the French. But Brant went into battle on the British side. The British finally won the war.

After the war, Brant went to work as Sir William's aide. Because he spoke English as well as his native language, Brant worked as an interpreter. He helped Sir William and the Iroquois to understand each other.

Sir William Johnson died in 1774. Brant then worked for Johnson's nephew, whose name was Guy Johnson. Together, Brant and Johnson went to England. They were trying to get Mohawk land back from the British. In return for the land, they promised that Mohawk warriors would fight on the side of the British in their war against the Americans. At that time, Americans were starting to fight for their independence from the British. This became the American War of Independence.

A **timeline** shows key events in the person's life.

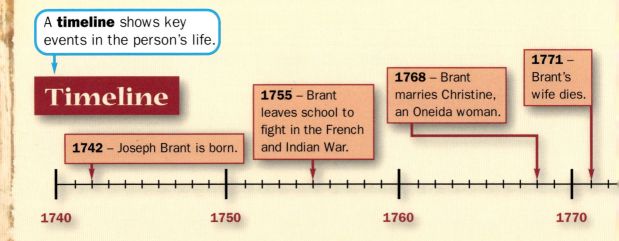

Timeline

1742 – Joseph Brant is born.

1755 – Brant leaves school to fight in the French and Indian War.

1768 – Brant marries Christine, an Oneida woman.

1771 – Brant's wife dies.

1740   1750   1760   1770

In 1776, the British made Brant a captain in the British Army. At the same time, the Mohawk made him a war chief. The American War of Independence had started. Brant led the Mohawk into war on the side of the British. He feared the Mohawk would lose their land if the British lost. Four Iroquois nations fought on the side of the British. However, two nations in the Iroquois League fought on the American side. This caused a split in the League.

In 1779, the four Iroquois nations and the British were defeated, and the Iroquois lost much of their land. Meanwhile, Brant helped the Americans bring about peace by helping them sign peace treaties with various groups.

Joseph Brant helped his people find new land for themselves. In 1784, some land along the Grand River in Ontario was given to the Mohawk, who settled down in many small villages along the river. The town, Brantford, Ontario, is named after Joseph Brant.

Brant was a well-educated man who was respected by both his people and Europeans. He is best remembered for trying to protect the land that he believed belonged to his people.

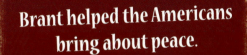

Brant helped the Americans bring about peace.

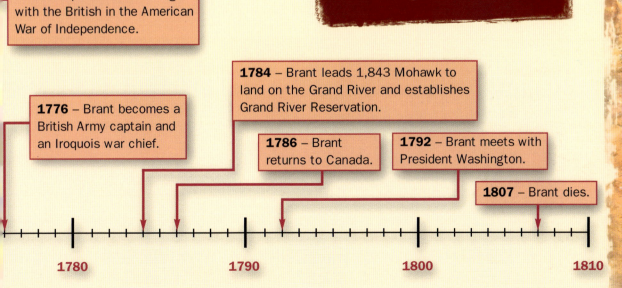

1775 – Brant persuades four of the Iroquois nations to fight with the British in the American War of Independence.

1776 – Brant becomes a British Army captain and an Iroquois war chief.

1784 – Brant leads 1,843 Mohawk to land on the Grand River and establishes Grand River Reservation.

1786 – Brant returns to Canada.

1792 – Brant meets with President Washington.

1807 – Brant dies.

1780   1790   1800   1810

Deskaheh (1872–1925)

Deskaheh

Deskaheh was born in 1872 on the Grand River Reservation. This was the reservation that Joseph Brant helped create. Deskaheh belonged to the Cayuga, one of the six Iroquois nations. After he finished high school, Deskaheh went to the United States and worked as a lumberjack in the Allegheny Mountains. Then he returned home to Grand River and took up farming. He married and had nine children.

Deskaheh was a great speaker and a representative for the Iroquois people. He could speak six Iroquois languages as well as English. He wanted to protect the rights of the Iroquois and spoke up for them when the Canadian government refused to grant the Iroquois the status of a separate nation. Because Canada was under British rule at this time, he decided to ask the British to safeguard his people's rights.

> Deskaheh was a great speaker and a representative for the Iroquois people.

Deskaheh traveled to England and asked to see King George V. However, he was not allowed to see the king. He was told that the British did not want to interfere with Canada's problems.

The Canadian government was not happy about Deskaheh's actions. They said Deskaheh was a troublemaker. He was forced to abandon his farm and leave the country.

In 1923, Deskaheh decided he would travel to Europe again, and ask for the support of the League of Nations. The League of Nations was a group of countries that had signed a pledge to work for peace. Deskaheh went to speak to delegates from other nations. However, he was denied the right to speak.

Before leaving, Deskaheh decided to hold a public meeting. Thousands of people came. Deskaheh was dressed in the traditional clothes of a chief of the Cayuga people. He told how his people had fought on the side of the British. In return, the British had given them Grand River Reservation. Yet now, he said, the promise was broken and the land was being taken back.

Deskaheh said he would not expect the people to believe his story without evidence. To back up his words, he showed the audience the sacred wampum belt that recorded the agreements Europeans had made with his people. Deskaheh translated the history recorded by the wampum so that the audience could understand.

Deskaheh decided he would travel to Europe again, and ask for the support of the League of Nations.

Deskaheh wearing western-style clothing

All of Deskaheh's hard work was making him ill. In 1925, he wanted to go home to Canada, but he was not allowed into the country. Instead, he went to the Tuscarora Reservation, which was in the United States. Deskaheh was sad that he could not go home and see his family. He was sad that governments had not listened to him. He died a disappointed man.

Deskaheh was sad that he could not go home and see his family.

Apply the Key Concepts

Key Concept 1 The homelands of native people have influenced their food, clothing, and shelter.

Activity

Choose three items the Iroquois found or hunted in their homeland. Make a sketch of each of these items using this book and other sources as references. Then use arrows and labels to tell how the Iroquois used these items in their daily lives.

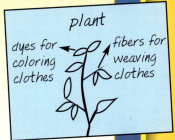

Key Concept 2 The stories and arts of native people were an expression of culture and a way of passing on values.

Activity

Culture is how a group of people carries out its traditions and way of life. Use four examples of Iroquois culture to create an Iroquois Cultural Handbook. First write a sentence or two for each topic. Then use images and descriptions from *The Iroquois* as guides for illustrating each topic. Make a cover for your handbook and remember to include the author's name!

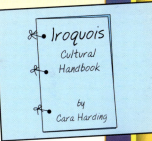

Key Concept 3 Early trade was a way of exchanging both goods and ideas.

Activity

Create a two-column chart listing the goods the Iroquois traded with other groups. Label the two columns: "Items the Iroquois Brought to Trade" and "Items the Iroquois Took Home." Include two or more items in each column.

Write Your Autobiography

Many people like to write autobiographies, or stories of their own lives. You can write a short autobiography that focuses on three or four important events in your life. You will probably have to do some research, though. Family members and friends can help you remember details.

1. Study the Model

Look back at pages 21–26. What are the things you need to think about when writing a biography or autobiography? You will need to remember these as you write your autobiography. Now, read one of the biographies again. As you read it, make a note of the most important events that are mentioned. Look at the timeline. Make a note of the important events on the timeline.

Writing an Autobiography

◆ Choose some important events in your life.

◆ Write about the events in the order that they happened.

◆ Use a timeline to chart important dates.

◆ Use pictures with captions to illustrate your autobiography.

2. Research Your Topic

You already know some important events in your own life. But there will be details about the events that you won't remember. You will need to ask your parents, grandparents, neighbors, and friends.

Make a list of the events that you want to include in your autobiography. Then make a list of questions to ask others. Take notes on what you learn. Try to get as many dates as possible so that you can create a timeline. You may also have some photographs that you can use to illustrate your autobiography.

3. Write a Draft

Look over all the information you have. Now look back at one of the biographies again. Use it to help you write about yourself. Then tell about your important events in order. If you wish, tell about how events made you feel or what you learned from them. Be sure to use pronouns like *I* and *me*. At the end, tie the events together in a concluding paragraph. Then draw up a timeline. Write a few words about the most important events along with the dates they occurred.

4. Revise and Edit

Read over your draft. What do you like? What would you like to change? Make these changes. Then read your draft again. This time, fix any mistakes. Look for words that are misspelled. Be sure each sentence starts with a capital letter. Be sure that you have your information in order.

Events in My Life

1. Got a new little sister

2. Rode my first bike

3. Was in the class play

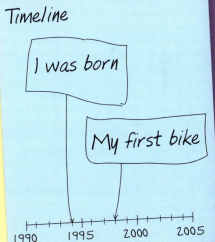

Timeline

I was born

My first bike

1990   1995   2000   2005

Publish Your Autobiography

Before you can share your autobiography, you need to publish it.

Take time to think about what your finished autobiography will look like. Do you have photographs? Where will they go? Can you keep these photographs or should you copy or scan them? Where will you put the timeline? What will you call your work? When you have made these decisions, write the final copy of your autobiography. Then you will be ready to share.

1. **Give your autobiography a title.** The title should include your name because your autobiography is your story. The title should also relate to the events you have written about.

2. **Include photographs or drawings.** Use photographs of yourself and your family, or illustrate your autobiography with your own drawings.

3. **Add captions to pictures.** Remember, captions and labels tell what pictures are about.

4. **Organize the events on a timeline.** Write a short description of the most important events next to their dates on your timeline.

Share Your Autobiography

Now you are ready to share your autobiography. Get together with a group of your classmates. Read each other's autobiographies. When you have all finished reading, discuss the things that are the same in your lives and the things that are different.

Glossary

breechcloth – a piece of cloth worn around the hips like a short skirt

culture – the traditions, language, dress, ceremonies, and other ways of life that a group of people share

expeditions – organized journeys in search of something

fertile – rich and good for growing crops

fibers – very fine, threadlike parts of plants that can be used to make cloth

goods – products that can be bought, sold, or exchanged

homeland – the place a people or nation chooses to make its home

league – a collection of different groups of people who work together to create peace

longhouses – long Native American houses built for large groups to live in

middlemen – people who buy goods and sell them again at a greater price

moccasins – soft leather shoes with soft soles

platforms – flat surfaces that are raised above the ground

trade – the buying, selling, or exchange of products

treaty – an official agreement between groups of people

wampum – beads made from shells strung into patterns with different meanings

Index